C000091870

Birmingham Repertory Theatre company presents
The World Premiere of

The Mother Ship

by **Douglas Maxwell**

First performed on 14 February 2008 at The Door, Birmingham Repertory Theatre

Then on tour at the following venues:
The Castle Hall, Hertford – 18 & 19 February
The Rhodes Arts Complex – 20 & 21 February
University of Hertfordshire – 22 February
Warwick Arts Centre – 29 February
The Door, Birmingham Repertory Theatre – 4 to 15 March
Arena Theatre, Wolverhampton – 19 March
Ludlow Assembly Rooms – 20 March
Traverse Theatre, Edinburgh – 25 to 29 March

As well as at schools and colleges throughout the West Midlands.

The tour is supported by The Sir Barry Jackson Trust

Birmingham Repertory Theatre
Centenary Square
Broad Street
Birmingham
B1 2EP
www.birmingham-rep.co.uk

The Mother Ship

By **Douglas Maxwell**

Eliot **Jonathan Bailey**
Gerry **Robert Ewens**
Judy **Robyn Hunt**
Lorraine **Joanne Moseley**
Kevin **Nicholas Oldale**
Macmillan **Daniel Settatree**

Director **Ben Payne**
Designer **Chloe Lamford**
Lighting Designer **Simon Bond**
Composer/Sound Designer **Jon Nicholls**
Stage Manager **Robin Longley**
Deputy Stage Manager **Olly Seviour**
Costume Supervisor **Debbie Williams**
Voice Coach **Catherine Weate**
Puppetry Advisor **Mervin Millar**
Extra Terrestrial Advisor **Professor Mark Brake**
Amphicar Advisor **David Chapman, Head of the UK Amphicar society**

With thanks to Lorna Laidlaw, David Birrell and Hattie Payne.

Biographies

Jonathan Bailey
Eliot

Theatre credits include: *Pretend You Have Big Buildings* (Royal Exchange Theatre); *Beautiful Thing* (Sound Theatre); *King John* (RSC); *Les Miserables* (Palace Theatre); *Les Enfants Du Paradis, A Christmas Carol* (RSC). Television credits include: *Golden Hour, Walk Away And I Stumble, Life Story Of Enzo Ferrari, The Bill, Doctors, Baddiel's Syndrome, Alice Through The Looking Glass, Bright Hair, Bramwell*. Film credits include: *St Trinians, Five Children And It, Permanent Vacation*.

Robert Ewans
Gerry

Robert is delighted to be taking his first professional role in *The Mother Ship*. After completing a first diploma in Performing Arts at Harlow College, performing in Willy Russell's *Our Day Out, Blood Brothers* and *Chicago*, he continued to work with a nearby arts organisation – Theatre Resource, Essex. Last year Robert won a place with Bradford-based theatre company Mind the Gap, on their 'Staging Change' course where he was one of six participants who visited 5 NCDT accredited London drama schools for actor training residencies, namely Mountview Academy of Theatre Arts, Arts Educational, Central School of Speech and Drama, Guildford School of Acting conservatoire and Oxford School of Drama. Robert is also a disability rights advocate.

Robyn Hunt
Judy

Training: BA (Hons) English, University of Plymouth. Theatre credits include: *The Whistle-Blower* for Birds of Paradise Theatre Company; *A Day Down A Goldmine, The Threepenny Opera, Oh, What A Lovely War!, Saame Sita, Asylum, Blacking Up, Nothing Ever Burns Down By Itself, Tamsin's Story, The Hogmanay Boys, Kaguyahime – The Moon Princess,* and *If I Die B4 U Wake* for Theatre Workshop. Will soon be appearing as Heide in *The First to Go* for Benchtours. Film credits include: *Crip Triptych* Sirius Productions.

Joanne Moseley
Lorraine

Training: Lamda. Theatre credits include: *Box, Forward, The Shooky, Transmissions* (Birmingham Repertory Theatre); *Of Mice And Men* (national tour, Birmingham Repertory Theatre, Savoy; nominated for best newcomer What's On Stage Award); *Silence* (tour and Birmingham Repertory Theatre); *Private Lives* (Birmingham Repertory Theatre); *The Crucible* (Leicester Haymarket). Television credits include: *Whistleblowers, The Rotters' Club, Doctors, Greenwing, People Like Us, Peak Practice, The Bill*. Radio includes: *Silver Street, The Archers, The Psychology Of Dangerous Roads*.

Nicholas Oldale
Kevin

Nicholas graduated from Central School of Speech and Drama/ Webber Douglas last July. Drama school productions included: *The Wedding Party, Saturday Sunday Monday, Live Like Pigs, Golden Girls, King Lear, 'tis Pity She's A Whore, The Importance*

Of Being Earnest, *Sexual Perversity In Chicago*, *Two Gentleman Of Verona*, *The Seagull*.

Daniel Settatree
Macmillan

Theatre credits include: *Transmissions* (Birmingham Repertory Theatre); *Gluey And The Lion*, Northern Exposure Festival (West Yorkshire Playhouse); *Dr Faustus* (Liverpool Everyman); *When My Heart Exploded* (Alma Tavern, Bristol); *Tony And Pat* (Leikin Loppu); *Angels In America* (Unity Theatre, Liverpool); *Edward II* (Cockpit Theatre); *Twelfth Night* (Theatre By The Lake, Keswick); *The Snow Queen* (Gateway, Chester); *The Humorous Lieutenant* (Battersea Arts Centre); *The Tempest* (Lincoln's Inn); *The Importance Of Being Ernest* (Swan, Worcester); *Macbeth* (Hull Truck); *Macbeth*, *When I Was A Girl I Used To Scream And Shout* (Swan, Worcester); *A Midsummer Night's Dream* (English Shakespeare Company); *Macbeth* (Creation Theatre Co. Oxford); *Edward II* (King's Head, London). Television credits include: UKTV Polar Season Promo, *Emmerdale*, *Twisted Tales*, *Outlaws*, *Poldark*. Radio credits include: *Children Of Witchwood*, *Parallel Paralysis*.

Douglas Maxwell
Author

Douglas Maxwell was born in 1974 in Girvan, a small town on the Ayrshire coast of Scotland. He is the author of many plays including *Decky Does A Bronco*, *Our Bad Magnet*, *Variety*, *If Destroyed True*, *Backpacker Blues*, *Melody* and *The Ballad of James II*. His work for young people includes *Helmet*, *Beyond* (with Nicola McCartney) and *Mancub*. He has also worked as Dramaturg with companies such as Highway Diner, Lung Ha's, East Glasgow Youth Theatre, Giant Productions and Random Accomplice. His plays have been performed in translation in Germany, Norway, Hong Kong, New York and South Korea, where *Our Bad Magnet* is in the midst of a three-year run. His plays are published by Oberon Books.

Ben Payne
Director

Ben Payne is Associate Director of Birmingham Repertory Theatre with particular responsibility for The Door, The REP's new writing theatre. For the company he has directed *Undercarriage* by David Watson, *Paradise* by Amber Lone, *Lifestock* and *The Seamstress' Revenge* with writer Michael Akraka and composer Jon Nicholls, and written adaptations of Jim Crace's novel *Quarantine* and Bertolt's Brecht's early play *The Wedding (Die Hochzeit)*. His play for young people *The Last Laugh* has been performed by youth theatres in the UK, Thailand, South Africa and New Zealand. His stage play and screenplay *On A Hiding To Nothing* written for Rideout Theatre Company and performed by excluded students from Lindsworth School in Birmingham, premiered at the New Vic Theatre, Stoke and Birmingham Film Festival. *Sinner* – a collaboration with dance theatre company Stan Won't Dance – toured the UK, Canada and USA 2004–2006 and was nominated for a Bessie Award in New York and a Dora Award in Canada. His adaptation of Joseph Moncure March's jazz age poem *The Wild Party* written for Rosie Kay Dance Company, toured nationally in 2007 and 2008. He is currently writing two new pieces of music theatre: *Unruly Music* and a play for children based on Camille Saint-Saëns' orchestral piece *The Carnival Of The Animals*.

Chloe Lamford
Designer

Chloe Lamford trained in Theatre Design at Wimbledon School of Art. She won best design at the 2007 TMA awards and was shortlisted for the Linbury Prize for set design in 2003. Design for theatre includes:

Small Miracle (Tricycle Theatre and Mercury Theatre, Colchester); *Blue Sky State* (Mercury Theatre, Colchester); *Antigone at Hell's Mouth* (National Youth Theatre and Kneehigh Theatre at the Soho Theatre); *Silence* (National Youth Theatre), Associate Designer to Es Devlin on *Gaddafi: A Living Myth* (ENO); *La Calisto* (Early Opera Company); *The Wild Party* (Rosie Kay Dance Company); *The Good Person Of Sichuan* (Birmingham), *Nine The Musical* (Arts Ed); *The Shy Gas Man* (Southwark Playhouse); *The Secret Ingredient, human/nature* and *Through The Walls* (Trestle Theatre Company); *Rough Cut* (Riverside Studios); *Holes And Wizzil* (Nuffield Theatre, Southampton). Chloe has also designed various shows for the Watford Palace Theatre including *Top Girls* (Main House), tours of *Mother Courage, Fear And Misery In The Third Reich, The Crucible*, and a site-specific project, *The Ring Road Tales*.She has designed various short films and music promos, and has written and directed a short film, *Being Venus*. Other work includes Art Director on Agent Provocateur's film starring Kate Moss, *The Four Dreams Of Miss X* directed by Mike Figgis. She also recently Production Designed *The Full Monteverdi*, an opera film for television. You can see Chloe's work at www.chloelamford.com.

Simon Bond
Lighting Designer

Simon began at Birmingham Repertory Theatre lighting shows for the Young REP and the annual Transmissions festival. He has since lit: *Katherine DeSouza, The Bolt Hole, The Santaland Diaries, The Laramie Project*, Decibel Festival, *Deadeye* and *A Thin Red Line* (Kali Theatre for Birmingham and Soho). Shows for Pentabus Theatre include *Strawberry Fields* (tour) and *White Open Spaces* (Edinburgh and Soho).

Jon Nicholls
Composer/Sound Designer

Jon studied composition at the London College of Music and electroacoustic music at Dartington, and over the past ten years has composed a huge range of music and sound scores for theatre, television and short film. He worked previously at The REP on *The Seamstress' Revenge* and *Katherine DeSouza*, and other theatre work includes *Silas Marner, Art, Blue Remembered Hills* and *The Changelings* (Theatr Clwyd); *Humble Boy* (Northampton Theatre Royal); *Much Ado About Nothing, Rosencrantz And Guildenstern Are Dead* and *Private Lives* (Manchester Library Theatre); *Amadeus* and *Masterclass* (Derby Playhouse); *Danny King Of The Basement* (Sheffield Crucible); *Oz* (Unicorn Theatre); *The Rivals, Alice In Wonderland* and *Thérèse Raquin* (Basingstoke Haymarket); and *Hansel And Gretel, Hamlet; First Cut, The Love Child, Nosferatu, Nicholas Nickleby, The Legend Of King Arthur, Get Carter* and *Vertigo* for Red Shift. Screen work includes the documentaries *Nuclear Ginza, Unwell, Women Facing War, Sex On The Streets, Spiked, Undercover Teacher, Running Dry* and *Why Kids Kill* for Channel 4 'Dispatches' and *We Can Be Heroes* for the BBC, and the short films *Lena, Shore, Little Boy Blues, Every Little Thing, Karain, The Hurlers, Kushe, My Constant Companion* and *The Havamal*. Music and sound design for radio drama includes *Between Friends, What I Heard About Iraq, Babel's Tower, Faust* and *Cat On A Hot Tin Roof* for Radio 3 and Radio 4, and he has also developed a series of live literature projects for voice and sound score; his most recent collaborations have been with the novelist Patrick Gale and the poet Jackie Kay and will be working with the poet Valerie Bloom in 2008. He is also a regular composer and performer of Javanese gamelan, and his opera *Falling Across* was premiered in 2006. For more information visit www.myspace.com/nichollsjon.

Birmingham Repertory Theatre Company

Sales Team
Anne Bower
Sharan Chauhan
Eileen Minnock
Jonathan Smith
Ryan Wootton

Senior Usher
Brenda Bradley
Thanks to our team of casual Box Office staff, ushers and firemen

Stage Door Reception
Tracey Dolby
Robert Flynn
Neil Hill
Julie Plumb

Building Services Officer
Colin Williamson

Building Services Assistant
John Usowicz

Cleaning
ISS Servisystem Midlands

Head of Production
Tomas Wright

Production Manager
Milorad Zakula

Production Assistants
Vicki Ayers
Hayley Seddon
(Maternity Cover)

Head of Stage
Adrian Bradley

Deputy Head of Stage
Kevin Smith

Stage Technicians
Guy Daisley
Mario Fortuin

Head of Lighting
Andrew Fidgeon

Deputy Head of Lighting
Phil Swoffer

Lighting Technician
Simon Bond

Head of Sound
Dan Hoole

Deputy Head of Sound
Clive Meldrum

Company Stage Manager
Ruth Morgan

Head of Workshop
Ed Cliff

Deputy Head of Workshop
Oliver Shapley

Carpenters/ Metalworkers/ Propmakers
Anthony Cowie
Michael Hurst

Acting Head Scenic Artist
Christopher Tait

Properties & Armourer
Alan Bennett

Head of Wardrobe
Sue Nightingale

Wardrobe Assistants
Lara Bradbeer
Melanie Francis
Brenda Huxtable
Debbie Williams

Head of Wigs & Make-Up
Andrew Whiteoak

Wigs & Make-Up Assistant
Jill Leather

With thanks to the following volunteers
Student REPresentatives

REP Archivist
Horace Gillis

⊞REP
Birmingham Repertory Theatre

Birmingham Repertory Theatre is one of Britain's leading national producing theatre companies. From its base in Birmingham, The REP produces over twenty new productions each year.

Artistic Director Rachel Kavanaugh has just announced her third season of work, which includes a new adaptation of Ibsen's *The Lady From The Sea*, Josie Lawrence in Stoppard's spy thriller *Hapgood*, Paul Lucas's new detective comedy *How To Tell The Monsters From The Misfits* and the musical *Our House*.

The commissioning and production of new work lies at the core of The REP's programme. The Door was established eight years ago as a theatre dedicated to the production and presentation of new writing. In this time, it has given world premieres to new plays from a new generation of British playwrights. The REP itself received The Peggy Ramsay Award for New Writing, enabling us to develop and commission more new plays for the future.

Developing new and particularly younger audiences is also at the heart of The REP's work, in its various Education initiatives, such as Transmissions, The Young REP, REP's Children, as well as with the programming of work in The Door for children.

The REP's productions regularly transfer to London and tour nationally and internationally. Recent transfers and tours have included *She Stoops To Conquer, To Kill a Mockingbird, Glorious!, The Birthday Party, The Witches, Through The Woods, Of Mice And Men, A Doll's House, The Crucible, Celestina, Hamlet, The Ugly Eagle, The Old Masters, The Snowman, The Gift, Behsharam (Shameless)* and *The Ramayana*.

Artistic Director Rachel Kavanaugh
Executive Director Stuart Rogers
Associate Director (Literary) Ben Payne

Book online at www.birmingham-rep.co.uk

Birmingham Repertory Theatre is a registered charity, number 223660

Birmingham City Council

European Community
European Regional
Development Fund

THE MOTHER SHIP

First published in 2008 by Oberon Books Ltd
521 Caledonian Road, London N7 9RH
Tel: 020 7607 3637 / Fax: 020 7607 3629
e-mail: info@oberonbooks.com
www.oberonbooks.com

The Mother Ship copyright © Douglas Maxwell 2008

A catalogue record for this book is available from the British
Library.

ISBN: 978-1-84002-833-1

Cover design by Fluid, www.fluidesign.co.uk

Printed in Great Britain by Antony Rowe Ltd, Chippenham.

cast

GERRY

A teenager with advanced support needs, 16.

ELIOT

His older brother, 18.

LORRAINE

Their stepmother, 30, if that. Pregnant.

MACMILLAN

A policeman.

KEVIN

Eliot's pal, 18.

JUDY

Uses a wheelchair, 18.

For my Dad George,
and my Daughter Ellis
who passed each other in the wings

1

A space mosquito

NEEEEEEEEAAAAAAAARRRRRRS

from the back of the universe.

It hovers. It zigs. It

HUZZZZZZZZZZZZZZZZZZZESS

Then after a moment of nothing, it sends out the call.

A call of sound. A call of light.

A light that tells Travellers:

The Mother Ship is leaving.

Soon, man, soon.

A light that zooms down from the stars to catch you in the eye.

Frozen in the beam.

Not scared though.

Happy.

Don't you get it? Didn't you hear?

It's home time.

At last.

2

ELIOT's getting nothing from GERRY's phone. Just a weird, buzzy, mosquitoy noise. He gives up and has another look at the envelope. Yup, it's still big and brown and sealed.

And absolutely terrifying.

When LORRAINE comes in with the cop he stuffs it under his shirt and puts on his best 'I Hate and Pity You' face.

LORRAINE is seriously stressed and seriously pregnant. She's been crying. The cop, MACMILLAN, seems awkward and out of his depth, struggling to be capable in the face of her panic.

LORRAINE Or there's this one. That was last year at Alton Towers but he's got sick all down him and his hair is different. If someone's photoshoping the hair could they do the sick as well? I don't want people thinking he's a puke-er, it was just that once. He's not a puke-er is he Eliot? Except that once.

MACMILLAN Ripsaw was it?

LORRAINE What?

MACMILLAN Was it the Ripsaw?

LORRAINE I don't know what you're saying. Is it police code? I've never done this before.

ELIOT You'll have to dumb down.

MACMILLAN There's a ride there called the Ripsaw. It can be very disorientating. I was violently ill on it last Easter Monday and I've very nearly got a pilot's licence so, a little fellow like your boy here could quite easily become…queasy, to say the least.

ELIOT He's not 'her boy'.

LORRAINE Or there's this one. I think this one's better. It's got the rest of his group from the day centre in it though. Will that cause confusion?

MACMILLAN   Are they all…em…they don't all look…to
the naked eye I mean…em…no this is fine.
Good, good…do you eh, have one with him
wearing what he was wearing this morning?

LORRAINE   I don't remember what he was wearing this
morning! Oh God. I can't even… I can't even
remember what he was wearing this morning.
I can't even do that.

MACMILLAN   Ah now, now. As I said before, nine times
out of ten these things are nothing to worry
about. He'll come tip-toeing in at tea time, tail
between his legs.

LORRAINE   But this is different…

ELIOT   In the sense that he doesn't really have a tail.

LORRAINE   It's not that he *shouldn't* have gone. It's that he
couldn't have gone. He's never gone anywhere
on his own. He just…can't. Sometimes I think
I'm cursed. I really am. I'm cursed.

ELIOT   And again, without warning, it's suddenly
about you.

LORRAINE   For God's sake Eliot I'm just trying to… He
doesn't speak for days and when he does it's
all side and teeth. If he thinks being a bitter
little smartarse is going to impress all those
university girls he's in for a shock.

ELIOT   What? I don't care about… I'm…university
girls are…and anyway, how would you know
about university girls?

LORRAINE   I know girls.

ELIOT   Not university girls.

LORRAINE   Girls are girls.

ELIOT   Some girls are thicker than others.

LORRAINE   See what I mean. He won't be happy till we're slapping each other on Jeremy Kyle.

MACMILLAN   Do you think he could be down at the day centre now?

ELIOT   Who, Jeremy Kyle? Wouldn't surprise me.

LORRAINE   No. He's not. They phoned me.

MACMILLAN   Maybe someone else picked him up? An extra-curricular activity or…?

LORRAINE   Drama! He does drama there. The woman that runs it had a nosebleed on *The X Factor* so now she's having a breakdown and taking it out on the theatre group.

MACMILLAN   Oh that's excellent. Not the nosebleed, the breakdown. Not the breakdown the eh…you know, the drama. It's what we in the force call 'a lead'.

LORRAINE   She'll've forgotten to tell me the timetable. I've got her number on my phone I think.

ELIOT goes to leave.

Where are you going?

ELIOT   Out.

LORRAINE   What for?

ELIOT   For what we in the force call 'a walk'.

LORRAINE   You can't.

ELIOT   I can. And until you let me use The Liberator, I'll have to won't I?

LORRAINE   You're not using The Liberator.

ELIOT   I'm 18! And you can't stop me. The keys are sellotaped behind that picture of Peter Duncan in the garage. I'm not dumb.

LORRAINE   I don't care if the keys are sellotaped to your face Elliot you're not taking it. The Liberator is Gerry's. It's his inheritance. You take it and I'll report it stolen.

ELIOT   I don't care.

LORRAINE   Yes you do. Your brother's missing.

ELIOT   That's right. *My* brother, *my* family. And while you and England's finest here chinwag about rollercoasters and puke, *I'm* going to find him.

LORRAINE   Eliot! Eliot!

He's gone.

I'm sorry.

MACMILLAN   No need. Happens all the time.

LORRAINE   I know what you're thinking. About me.

MACMILLAN   Eh…do you?

LORRAINE   You think I'm a screaming mess. An unfit mother. That it's all my fault.

MACMILLAN   (*Relief.*) Oh. Right. Good. I mean, no. I don't think that at all.

LORRAINE   I'd agree with you if you did.

MACMILLAN   Oh don't say that. You set yourself off in a spiral saying stuff like that. I mean, I may have doubts about the standard of my policing, but you won't hear me say a word aloud, for fear of spiralling. Did you…eh… notice anything about it by the way? My policing. Anything a little bit crap?

LORRAINE Well. Not really.

MACMILLAN Oh good. Because sometimes I think I'm not 100 per cent brilliant at it. I seem to inspire sarcasm and often struggle to get results. They make me work alone you see, so I'm never really sure about the right thing to do in any given situation.

LORRAINE So…you're saying that you're probably not going to find Gerry?

MACMILLAN Well, realistically, someone else will find him. Or he'll just turn up. Or…

LORRAINE Or what?

MACMILLAN I shouldn't have said that last 'or'. I add 'ors'. That's another thing.

LORRAINE Oh Jesus. Look I'm not over-reacting. He's… it's not just that he's got needs, he's got ideas too.

MACMILLAN Ideas?

LORRAINE Yeah.

MACMILLAN What kind of ideas?

LORRAINE Well…he…he thinks… he's under the impression…he…no. It's nothing. Don't listen to me, I'm just, you know.

MACMILLAN Teenagers eh?

LORRAINE Yeah. And they're going through a hard time. We lost their dad three months ago. Cancer.

MACMILLAN Cancer? God that's funny.

LORRAINE Is it?

MACMILLAN   Well my dad died when I was at school.
            Cancer. Same thing. Amazing eh? Small
            world.

LORRAINE   Yeah. And what with… (*Rubs her belly.*) …it's
           been difficult.

MACMILLAN   Yup. And I tell you what, it's going to get a
            lot worse before it gets better. Behaviour wise.
            Oh yes. I went *right* off the rails. Grief can
            manifest itself in strange ways. Especially for
            youngsters. For me it was plane-spotting. I
            was fifteen at the time, very upset, obviously,
            and before I knew what was happening I was
            deeply involved in the plane-spotting scene.
            Deeply involved. I'm still into aviation of
            course, but I resist the lure of 'the spot'. I can
            nearly fly a helicopter. Not long now. Get
            the old stomach under control. But no, the
            plane-spotting days were dark and confusing.
            Eventually my mum had to get a lock for my
            door. She was convinced I'd fail all my exams
            if I continued down that weird path to…

LORRAINE   What did you say?

MACMILLAN   Oh yes it's a weird path. A weird and
            terrifying…

LORRAINE   No. Exams. Exams! Oh God. Look I have
           to go.

MACMILLAN   Where are we going?

LORRAINE   To get results.

3

Some of that goddamn bedroom music.

It's KEVIN's room and he is raging. He paces like a lawyer in a film. He doesn't look like a lawyer though. He's still wearing his uniform from work. A bright yellow T-Shirt with 'LIFEGUARD' printed on it. Come to think of it, he doesn't look much like a lifeguard either.

ELIOT is lying back on the bed reading a crumpled letter.

KEVIN So he comes limping into the Sunken Tsunami Zone, his trucking toad face all, like, toading out all over the joint. I was like, 'What does this daft bar steward want now?' So he starts screaming all like 'I know it was you McCloy'. And I was like 'Prove it'. So he turns round and says 'I don't need to prove it. I know it was you that wrote the letter, so pack your flipflops and hit the bricks.' 'No way,' I goes, 'this is unfair dismissal. I've been a lifeguard at this pool since before I could swim. You chuck me out and I'm going to tribunal. Where's your proof?' He says 'No proof necessary. I can tell you wrote it from the language.'

ELIOT (*Reading.*) 'Dear Dicks, Any dick that goes to this meeting is a dick.' And it's signed, 'Mr and Mrs Piss'.

KEVIN So I says 'Well that's where you're wrong Toadteeth, 'cos I don't swear'.

ELIOT Except that you do.

KEVIN Not anymore.

ELIOT Yeah right.

KEVIN Nope. I've changed it.

ELIOT   What do you mean?

KEVIN   I've changed it. I was up all night
reprogramming my linguistic hard-drive.
He'll never trip me up. I'll show him. Little
toad faced motherfunster. I'll never swear
again.

ELIOT   Oh so that's why you're talking funny.

KEVIN   It's not funny, it's deadly serious old boy. I've
a whole new dictionary of filth at my disposal
and they can't touch me for it. They won't
even know I'm swearing. Listen…truck off,
trucker, truckface, truckstick, brick, brickhead,
bar steward, pass, pass hole, pass licker, mid
Atlantic oil tanker, and of course the king of
all swearwords…constable.

ELIOT   You'll never keep it up.

KEVIN   That's what they said to Girls Aloud, and look
at them now.

ELIOT   So you're sacked?

KEVIN   Sacked? I'm suing *them* for unfair harassment.
And now that I don't swear they'll have
to cave and I'll be in the mint. He's got
absolutely no proof that I wrote that letter.

ELIOT   Even though you did.

KEVIN   He doesn't know that.

ELIOT   Well, he accused you.

KEVIN   Out of the blue.

ELIOT   Of something that you actually did.

KEVIN   Because he hates me.

ELIOT   Or because you actually did it.

KEVIN   Whose side are you on ya pritt-sticking son of a ditch?

ELIOT   No way are you keeping that up.

KEVIN   Fiver. Oh yeah talking about being a pritt-stick, you seen this? Ripped it off the notice board down at the centre, especially for you.

ELIOT   What is it?

A poster.

KEVIN   Read it.

ELIOT   'Virginity Now. A conference for all school leavers heading off to university to discuss the Christian ideal of abstinence.' The House of Light? Never heard of it.

KEVIN   I thought 'My mate E's a sad virgin Christian loser heading off to uni. Perfect.'

ELIOT   I'm not a Christian.

KEVIN   You went to Sunday school.

ELIOT   When I was about seven.

KEVIN   Once a sad virgin Christian loser, always a sad virgin Christian loser. Well if you don't want it I'll have it. Might pop in and lure some young Jedi over to the dark side.

ELIOT   And anyway, I might not be going to uni.

KEVIN   Nah man, you're a bright spark. Get the funk out of this tiny dump, hit the city and never come back. That's what I'd do. You get your results?

ELIOT   Not yet.

KEVIN   Any day now eh?

ELIOT Yeah. Anyway, I'm thinking about getting a job.

KEVIN Where?

ELIOT I hear there might be an opening down at the swimming pool.

KEVIN (*Dry.*) Ha ha.

ELIOT Hey you never saw Gerry down at the centre did you?

KEVIN Gerry? Yeah. Think so.

ELIOT Knew it. The Step is going ape man.

KEVIN What now?

ELIOT She's got it in her head that Gerry's done a bunk. Got the cops in. As if.

KEVIN She's a heavy panic merchant. She's losing it. Sooner you get out of there the better mate.

ELIOT Yeah. So I said I'd track him down. Get her off my back. Thought I'd pop in. See if there's any leads.

KEVIN She's…you need to totally get out of there man.

ELIOT Totally.

KEVIN Think it was him. He was with that girl.

ELIOT What girl?

KEVIN That one in the wheelchair he bumps about with. Nah it was definitely him. Almost certainly definitely.

ELIOT Ah, I'd better get down there.

KEVIN Cool. I'll come too. I want that toad faced dock plunger to get a load of my new lingo.

ELIOT Hey, you know constable isn't the king of all swearwords. I've got one better. After Gerry's accident right, Dad wouldn't let anyone say words like spastic or spaz or mongo or Joey or anything like that, know what I mean? So me and Gerry made up our own word. One word to rule all others.

KEVIN What was it?

ELIOT Moonster. And moonster is definitely the king of all swearwords.

4.

JUDY lolls in her chair and gargles. Flails the limbs and judders.

Eyes roll. Not just hers, but ELIOT and KEVIN's too.

They're getting nowhere with this. Wait a minute, she's trying to say something…

JUDY I…go…need… (*Muffled.*) chocolate.

KEVIN What's she on about?

ELIOT I dunno.

KEVIN WHAT…ARE…YOU…ON…ABOUT?

JUDY I…go…need.

ELIOT She needs something.

KEVIN You do it. You're up on this stuff.

ELIOT What stuff?

KEVIN Moonsters and stuff.

ELIOT Kevin!

KEVIN What?

ELIOT   Look, we just want to know if you've seen Gerry? Gerry? Your mucker Gerry? Nup. Lights are on but…

KEVIN   I don't even think the lights are on. I think the whole street's had the electricity switched off for some time now.

ELIOT   Jesus Christ Kev.

KEVIN   Easy on the blasphemy, Toad's lurking.

ELIOT   Just…shut it then. Judy? Judy do you remember your little pal Gerry? Well I'm his brother. Bru-ther.

JUDY   Brrr…

ELIOT   That's right, brother. Good girl. Very good. You're a clever girl.

JUDY   I go…need chocolate.

ELIOT / KEVIN   (*Understanding at last.*) Aaaaaaaaw.

ELIOT   Go and get her some chocolate will you?

KEVIN   Me?

ELIOT   You work here.

KEVIN   Oh so I'll just open the vending machine with my supersonic locker key then eh? I work in the pool it's totally different.

ELIOT   Oh for…if it's the dosh…

JUDY   Na! Na. I…need…make chocolate.

ELIOT   Make chocolate?

JUDY points to her trousers.

KEVIN   Oh shysters…

ELIOT   You don't make chocolate, you eat chocolate. Yuuummmm.

KEVIN   No, Eliot man, scarper. Run away! She's... she's making chocolate in her pants. She's making pant chocolate!

ELIOT   Eh? Oh my God. Oh my God. Where are you going?

KEVIN   I've just remembered I've got some work guff I need to... I forgot to file some...verrucas... I'll check in back at the ranch make sure you got Gerry back safe and sound, okay dude? Adios.

And he's off.

ELIOT   Kevin! Kev! Get back here you...you... constable. Oh God.

ELIOT starts to wheel JUDY about in a panic looking for help/the toilets. She starts to raise the pitch of her groaning.

JUDY   Need it NOW!

ELIOT   Okay, hold it in. Hold in the chocolate and I'll get some help.

JUDY   Chocolate!

ELIOT   I need the ladies' toilets! Where are the ladies' toilets?

JUDY   (*Getting distressed.*) Chocolate! Chocolate!

ELIOT   No! No chocolate! (*Shouting.*) Hey! Help! Help! If I don't get into the ladies' toilets soon I'm going to like, totally freak out! Ladies' toilets! Ladies' toilets!

JUDY   Chocolate! Chocolate!

ELIOT No chocolate! No chocolate! No, no, no, no, no, no, no!

JUDY produces a packet of Rolos from her trouser pocket.

JUDY Okay suit yourself. More for me. (*Pops one in her mouth.*) Mmmm. God I love a Rolo.

ELIOT (…) Eh?

JUDY 'I need to get into the ladies' toilets! I'm going to like, totally freak out! Ladies' toilets!' Ha ha ha. Dick.

ELIOT What? What?

JUDY I can't believe you're Gerry's brother. He's so, like, cool and you're like, so not. (*About the Rolos.*) Oh, last one.

She chucks the last Rolo at ELIOT without any real malice. It bounces off his chest. He barely notices…

ELIOT That's…that's… You were pretending to be…you were…oooh that's so bad. That's ultra heavy bad man. I, for one, am appalled.

JUDY Hey I just give my audience what they crave. I'm a brilliant actress. Watch this, 'To be or not to be…'

ELIOT Not to be. Definitely not to be.

JUDY Ah chill out fool. You're only embarrassed 'cos you saw the chair and assumed I was a…what was the word…moonster? Did they teach you that at Idiot School or was that something you and the sidekick came up with one night when you were lying in bed cuddling?

ELIOT I…just… Shut up.

JUDY If you're looking for Gerry you're too late. He's gone.

ELIOT Gone? You mean he's not here?

JUDY You must be the brains of the outfit. Yes he's away.

ELIOT What do you mean away? Away where? How can he be away?

JUDY By not being here.

ELIOT You're saying he's not here? He left? On his own?

JUDY God it's like talking to a talented dog. And by the way, no, I didn't say he was on his own. He took some of his drama group with him. I think Stunned Aaron and little Rosie tagged along too.

ELIOT Where?

JUDY Ah now there's the rub. Nobody knows. It was his secret. He wanted to tell me but I said 'Gerry, if it's your secret, then guard it. Just go, and don't trust men who run down stairs with their hands in their pockets.'

ELIOT You just stood there…

JUDY Sat there.

ELIOT Sat there, and let a kid with advance support needs walk out the… I mean where were the carers? Does the centre know? Do the police know? Does anyone…when was this…?

JUDY He's sixteen years old.

ELIOT He can't just leave. Don't you get it? He can't. Jesus Christ. If I find out you put him up to

this I swear to God. You'd better hope he's
alright.

ELIOT goes to leave.

JUDY He said the Space Mosquito came back. It
gave him the signal. He said The Mother Ship
is leaving and he has to go home. I wonder
what he means?

ELIOT freezes. Suddenly stricken and miles away.

Like a zombie, he exits.

*JUDY pretends that she doesn't feel guilty, but can't quite
shake it off. Maybe she should have stopped GERRY after
all? Or maybe she should go after ELIOT?*

*Before she can do anything though, LORRAINE and
MACMILLAN enter in a rush. LORRAINE crosses the
stage looking for someone official, she's mid panic.
MACMILLAN comes over to JUDY.*

MACMILLAN Hello my little darling. Hey I've got a big
question for a little girl like you, do you
think you can understand it if I speak slowly?
Okaydoaky. Where…is…the…office?

After a moment.

JUDY I…go…need…chocolate.

5

Outside and ELIOT wants to run.

He tries to, but he can't.

He's stuck. Way, way back there.

Back when he came up with the whole thing.

Back when seeing little GERRY in tears and bleeding made his ribcage catch fire.

He was only a kid then too. People forget that.

Back when his dad had told him to 'look after your brother, no-matter what'.

That was what he was doing. Right?

ELIOT Who was it?

GERRY All of them. They were singing a song Eliot.

ELIOT All of them? Where was Father Archie?

GERRY They were singing a song and I tried to do what you said, but I fell, and they were laughing.

ELIOT Are you…you'll be alright. Hear me? Stop crying, ya big baby. You're fine.

GERRY No. Look. That's my blood.

ELIOT So? Blood's just blood. Look. There's my blood and I'm not crying.

GERRY I'm not as good. I'm not as good. I'm worse. They said I'm broken. I'm a worse boy.

ELIOT What? Who…? Shut up you moonster. I've told you this. You're *better.*

GERRY I'm not though.

ELIOT Yeah. Everything about you's better than them. Than anyone.

GERRY Is it? No.

ELIOT Yeah. You're different right, but in a, like, amazing way, or something.

GERRY How?

ELIOT   'Cos…'cos… Right I'm not meant to tell you this okay, so promise to keep it a secret. A super, super, heavy secret. Don't even tell Dad right? Promise?

GERRY   Mmmhhmm.

ELIOT   Hope to die.

GERRY   Tell me Eliot.

ELIOT   Spit.

GERRY   Tell me!

ELIOT   It explains everything right; how you're different now, how people are weird to you and eh…how…how everything. It's about where you come from.

GERRY   I know where I come from.

ELIOT   Where you *really* come from.

And here he is again, in the present and all alone.

And where you're really going.

ELIOT slumps to the ground, lost in thought, head in hands.

6

Skypods change the world

With the stroke of a smooth white dial

Everything goes clear, ordered, digital.

Charting a 3-D laser blue course through the country

tttttttrrr----tttttttrrr----tttttttrrr----tttttttrrr

Not far now.

This map is easy.

Stay true crew. Follow on.

This way!

Then there's a

THRUUUUUMMMMMM

Eyes glow.

All eyes glow.

You know what that means.

That means there are other Travellers close by.

Send out a search call.

There it goes,

Bounce bing bop

Like a pinball popping

Faster faster faster till

There they are.

Stranded and huddled.

Travellers all. And found now.

Hearts lift.

Eyes glow.

They're to be saved. They're going home.

But first there's the Guard.

A terrifying shadow creature that has them trapped.

When you come this far, you don't leave anyone behind.

Draw weapons. Deep breath.

Yell the Traveller Yell.

Attack!

7

In the ramshackle office of Sundrenched Leisure and Care facilities. LORRAINE has had no answers and her panic has crossed over into a calm sorrow. She seems older somehow and sips tea from a plastic cup.

MACMILLAN has been electrified. He's hanging up on an important call. The stakes have been raised.

MACMILLAN Right. Well. It's definite. Driver says the mini-bus was taken about an hour ago. It was definitely Gerry and his mates.

LORRAINE Gerry can't drive. He can hardly…it can't be him.

MACMILLAN I'll save you from the description but there's no mistake. The driver says he had stopped the bus for what he categorises as 'a slash', Gerry appeared out of nowhere with two associates…em…a ray gun was produced…

LORRAINE A what?

MACMILLAN At which point the passengers of the bus (nine young people with varying degrees of physical and learning difficulties) started to glow…

LORRAINE What?

MACMILLAN No sorry, that's my mistake.

LORRAINE Thank God for that.

MACMILLAN Their *eyes* started to glow…

LORRAINE *Their eyes star…*?

MACMILLAN An invisible force field then pitched the driver into a hedge where he suffered minor scratches and an unspecified animal bite while the kids made their escape in the vehicle.

LORRAINE Was this guy drunk?

MACMILLAN Well he's drunk now that's for sure, but apparently at the time he was stone cold sober.

LORRAINE This is ridiculous.

MACMILLAN Yes it does seem a bit odd. Either that or…

LORRAINE What?

MACMILLAN Nothing.

LORRAINE Stop adding 'ors'. Look, my stepson is in a minibus with a group of strangers, flying off to God knows where, driven by God knows who, wanting God knows what. They need spotting, they need saving.

MACMILLAN Or, maybe people need saving *from* them.

LORRAINE It's a bus of kids with special needs. What are they going to do?

MACMILLAN Can I remind you they have at least one ray gun.

LORRAINE Ah but you see, they don't though do they? That's made up.

MACMILLAN Yes. You'd hope.

LORRAINE You don't need to hope. There's no such thing as a ray gun.

MACMILLAN   Yeah. I know. Correct. Or phasers. They're
three years from readiness. At least. Don't
worry, we're all over this mess like…em…
like…em.

JUDY   Like a professional police force searching for
missing children?

MACMILLAN   Exactly. The county is covered. They can't
and they won't get far. And on the bright side,
it doesn't have the hallmarks of a hostage
situation. Yet.

LORRAINE   Oh my God.

MACMILLAN   There's nothing more to be done here. The
day centre are in a flat-spin and freaking
out. Helps no one. And was it just me or did
that guy actually *look* like a toad to you? Not
important. I'll drop you off at home, get to
the station and we'll have Gerry back for
bedtime. The Governor reckons if it wasn't
for me they wouldn't have put two and two
together on this. Wants me in there pronto.
'Good work' he said. That's a first.

LORRAINE   No look, you get to your desk. I'll walk. It's
two minutes and I need the time. I've got my
phone. The tiniest thing, call.

MACMILLAN   Absolutely. Constant updates. Here's my
card. Em… I'll write my home number on it.
Just in case.

LORRAINE   Just in case what?

MACMILLAN   Well…I don't know. Just in case you…fancy
a ride in a helicopter or…or… Right. I'd
better… Try not to get too stressed. Bad for
the baby.

LORRAINE Wait, (*Reading from the card.*) Constable…
Constable? Your name's Constable? Constable
Constable.

MACMILLAN Like the painter. Macmillan Constable.

LORRAINE Jesus that must make life…

MACMILLAN Yes. It doesn't help. Call me Mac. Please.

LORRAINE puts the card in her pocket.

LORRAINE Look there is something else I wanted to tell
you. You see Gerry plays a kind of…game,
where he…

*KEVIN enters, shouting back at someone unseen. He
doesn't notice LORRAINE or MACMILLAN.*

KEVIN Well that's where you're wrong Toadster,'cos
I'm suspended till Wednesday and free time
is way beyond your jurisdiction. And even if I
did startle that fat cow, at no point did I curse,
swear or blaspheme, so point your axis of evil
at some other sucker and start thinking about
getting yourself a good lawyer, Toadboy,
you're going to need one.

LORRAINE What the hell are you doing here? Where's
Eliot?

KEVIN is changed.

KEVIN Lorraine. You're glowing.

LORRAINE There's a lot of it about. What's going on?

KEVIN I work here. In the pool. I was just looking
for a C1-14 Internal Complaint form. I'm
bringing down the system from within. Again.
And who might this be?

LORRAINE   This is Const…this is a policeman, so show some respect. And don't call me Lorraine either, I've told you.

MACMILLAN   There was something else?

LORRAINE   No it's okay. Just find him. Please. Go.

MACMILLAN   Are you sure you're…?

KEVIN   She's told you once now on your way.

LORRAINE   Kevin!

MACMILLAN   I'll keep you up to speed. And I'm sure someone will…no…I'm sure *I'll* find him. I promise. Lorraine.

LORRAINE   Thank you Mac.

MACMILLAN smiles and slowly goes. He gives a hesitant glance towards KEVIN who bats it back harshly with a glare.

KEVIN   I thought he'd never leave. Alone at last. Sorry about the mess. Toad's a pig. Should be me in here. I was overlooked for the promotion because of my radical political ideas. That and the incident with the waste pipe in the paddling pool. But one day, all this could be ours.

LORRAINE   Oh for God's sake don't start.

KEVIN   I know this is a difficult time for you Lorraine, but I'm here to support you. To comfort you. To hold you.

LORRAINE   Kevin I can't take any more of your bloody nonsense. Gerry's missing and Eliot's gone and…and…

KEVIN   Sssshhhh…ssshhhhh……there there.

He holds her shoulders. She…

LORRAINE   Touch me again and I swear I will rip your arm off and force it back into your body in the worst possible way.

KEVIN   I've written you another poem.

LORRAINE   Oh Jesus Christ.

KEVIN   ''Twas on the funeral morn when we first kissed…'

LORRAINE   We have never kissed! You leant in and lingered and I…it was a linger. It was absolutely nothing. It was nothing!

KEVIN   'And since that day my heart doth miss, her fingertips, and the pounding heave of her worldly…' I can't say the last bit because I don't swear anymore and Toads have ears. But you get the gist. It goes on…

LORRAINE   Right I'm out of here. I can't handle this. You're an idiot and a pest and a…a…

KEVIN   What are you trying to say Lorraine?

LORRAINE   I'm trying to say I don't want you anywhere near me. I'm trying to say I never want to see your ridiculous face ever again.

She leaves the office and hustles outside, followed on her coattails by KEVIN. Neither of them see ELIOT sitting where we left him. Head in hands.

KEVIN   I know you don't mean that. Because I do remember our first kiss, and I remember holding you and I remember kissing you. And you kissing me back. I love you Lorraine. I love you.

LORRAINE   Eliot!

ELIOT   What's…?

KEVIN   Eliot mate. Look I can explain. You see, I'm… I'm… I am, to all intents and purposes…your new dad.

LORRAINE / ELIOT   *What?*

Commotion. ELIOT turns and runs.

LORRAINE   (*Shouting after him.*) Eliot! Ignore him he's a…how did you get on in your exams? I've been worried… I've been…

KEVIN   No Lorraine. Let him go.

KEVIN holds LORRAINE back as she tries to follow ELIOT off, like he's seen people do in soap operas. After a beat, she turns on him violently, all the frustrations of the day pour out in punches.

ELIOT stops dead. Changes his mind. He's not going home. He's going somewhere else.

JUDY saw the whole thing. She follows him.

8

A row of lock up garages.

ELIOT arrives gasping for breath for a number of very good reasons. He pulls his keys from his pocket.

His mind is made up. He's on his own now and on a mission. He goes to the least loved garage door, and begins a sore-looking wrestling match with it, the door taking most of the points.

After a while the door screeches up. Inside is a car covered in a tarpaulin. ELIOT whips off the tarpaulin to reveal an old, weird-looking convertible.

*He stands apart from the car, as if he's afraid of it, or
of something else: the memory of it. He shrugs it off.
After rescuing the keys from behind a picture of Peter
Duncan he climbs in and starts it up. He gets nothing
but hard noise.*

*The place is starting to fill with black smoke by the time
JUDY appears.*

JUDY Did you see me go? I was like, zoom! Flames
from the spokes man. I could've been an
athlete you know. Unfortunately I tested
positive for having a personality the day
before the race and had to pull out. Thought
I'd have to pull out there too, if you'd gone
any further. So anyhoo, I was thinking, about
where Gerry was heading and what you
said and stuff. And I remembered. He gave
me a picture with some words written on it.
Yesterday. Hear me? Might be a… Is that
your car? Do you want me to phone Pimp
My Ride?

ELIOT It's not a car.

JUDY Looks like a car.

ELIOT Well it's not. It's an Amphicar. It's my
inheritance. Sorry, *Gerry's* inheritance. We call
it The Liberator and if you don't watch out
it's going to monstertruck right over you.

JUDY Can you drive it?

ELIOT We're going to find out aren't we.

At last the engine starts and splutters into smoky life.

JUDY Wait! Eliot. I might know where he's going.
Gerry gave me a clue. I think we can find
him.

After a long moment.

40

ELIOT This is where you tell me what the clue is.

JUDY Here?

ELIOT Oh sorry, where would you prefer, Vegas?

JUDY Can't I tell you in the whatdoyoucallit? The Libertine Amphicar thing?

ELIOT Why?

JUDY I dunno. Just.

ELIOT Well…no.

JUDY Oh. Well I don't think I'll tell you at all then. Probably not important.

ELIOT What…why would you…?

JUDY I'll be offski and say ta ta.

She starts to go.

ELIOT I can't believe…look…oh for Christ's sake! Right okay.

JUDY What really?

ELIOT Yes.

JUDY Ooooh.

ELIOT Jump in then.

JUDY lets ELIOT work out on his own that she can't do that. Finally, and cursing under his breath, ELIOT gets out and lifts her, and then her chair into the car.

It's a weirdly awkward moment and both of them know it. Halfway between a dance move and something else.

Once they're in, ELIOT, shaking his head and muttering, guns it, and The Liberator disappears in a coughing fit of black exhaust.

A few moments later LORRAINE and KEVIN run in, or as close as they can come to running. KEVIN holds a hankie to his bleeding nose. LORRAINE speaks to the fading exhaust.

LORRAINE Please! Come home.

KEVIN You know, I can't help but feel partly responsible for this.

After drawing KEVIN the mother of all glares she gets out MACMILLAN's card, sighs, and calls the number.

9

ELIOT and JUDY are put-put-putting along in the Amphicar. ELIOT, anything but comfortable behind the wheel, is glued to the road, knuckles white.

JUDY Shouldn't you have L plates on?

No response.

You've passed your test right?

Nothing.

What about your exams, have you passed your exams?

Even less of a response.

I have. Passed my exams last year. Passed them so much that when the certificate came back it just had one word printed on it: 'genius'. You don't need qualifications in my game. Thanks for asking. I'm a writer. Gonna be.

ELIOT Shut up, where am I going?

JUDY Don't drive antsy. Be the road.

ELIOT   Where am I going?

JUDY   How am I meant to know?

ELIOT   You said you knew where he was.

JUDY   I said I *might* know where he was. At best it's a clue. At worst it's a squiggle.

ELIOT   You said…

JUDY   Eyes on the road.

ELIOT   You said…

JUDY   No I didn't. He made me a picture. Before he left. And he's never done that before. I thought 'Ah ha! Maybe Gerry's leaving me directions in his own sweet little Gerry way.'

ELIOT   For God's sake. What's the picture of?

She unfolds the picture and nearly loses it in the wind.

What is it?

JUDY   I don't know. A big tower? An arrow?

ELIOT   It looks like…

JUDY   Road!

ELIOT   It looks like a Christmas tree.

JUDY   If you almost completely shut your eyes. I suppose. A little bit.

ELIOT   A little bit? That's a definite Christmas tree. (*Smiling for the first time.*) And I know where he's going. Every year my Dad used to take us all up to this field where they planted old Christmas trees right? Like, recycled them. We'd scale the wire and steal our tree.

JUDY   I love a traditional family Christmas.

43

ELIOT   We wouldn't really steal it. Found out years
        later that he was pals with the farmer. But
        when we were nippers it was the biggest buzz
        ever. Mum used to pretend she was scared
        that something would happen and crouch
        in the backseat. Then, after, it was a place
        we'd go to think about her. And remember
        stuff. Just the three of us left in The Liberator.
        That's where he is. That's where Gerry is
        now.

JUDY   And what about this Mother Ship thing, is
        that with the Bootleg Christmas trees too?

ELIOT   Forget that! This has got nothing to do with
        the Mother Ship. Nothing.

JUDY   Oooooooh. One last question then I promise
        to shut it.

ELIOT   Don't make promises you can't keep.

JUDY   If an Amphicar isn't really a car, what is it?

ELIOT   An amphibious vehicle.

JUDY   You mean it can fly!

ELIOT   No. I mean it can go on the water.

JUDY   What... This can turn into a boat?

ELIOT   It doesn't turn into a boat. It *is* a boat.

JUDY   *And* a car?

ELIOT   Yes.

JUDY   You mean you could drive this into a lake and
        it would sail away?

ELIOT   Yes.

JUDY   Like James Bond?

ELIOT Yes.

JUDY But that's not real.

ELIOT Well this one's real 'cos you're sitting in it.

JUDY Wait a minute, go back. This car drives on water?

ELIOT Yes! Jesus Christ! They're called Amphicars. There was about 5000 made in the sixties. There's only seven in Britain and this is one of them. My dad was head of the Amphicar Society. He crossed the channel in 1986. It was on *Blue Peter* and everything. He called this one The Liberator and don't ask me why 'cos I don't know.

JUDY Oh my God. This is so cool. Let's play with it! Let's play with it! We have to drive it on water immediately! For proof.

ELIOT You're not allowed to play with it. No one is. That's why he left it to Gerry. I think. He'd never use it. So nothing can happen. But I'm totally allowed to take it. Totally. It probably doesn't work now anyway. It hasn't been on water since…and listen, I've got plenty of proof. There's a photo I've got, right. It's my mum and dad at the seaside. They're miles out to sea and the Amphicar looks silver 'cos it's nearly night. It was their first date. And mum's eyes are brighter than the spotlight behind her. Dad's laughing so hard. And everything about the whole scene looks so…impossible. But real at the same time. Know what I mean? I love that picture. We both do. So there *is* proof. I've got proof.

After a while.

JUDY Do you think we should…?

ELIOT No! I don't want to get into… I don't want them to… He's my brother. He's my brother and I'll find him.

JUDY I was going to say do you think we should get some L-plates, 'cos you obviously don't really know how to drive do you?

ELIOT I've had three tests.

JUDY And how many have you passed?

ELIOT Nearly one.

JUDY Yeah, this is just like James Bond. In a not really kind of way.

10

LORRAINE sits with MACMILLAN in GERRY's bedroom. The walls are covered in drawings and paintings of spaceships and planets. Lots of NASA stuff and a telescope.

MACMILLAN's taking a statement but sometimes the pen falls to the pad, lost, like the rest of him, in LORRAINE's eyes: sad and perfect and miles away.

LORRAINE Jim encouraged it. It was a giggle at the start and Gerry was so passionate about it, which is something to see I tell you. Now he knows it freaks people out, so it's something secret he keeps to himself. Usually. He talks to me about it. Most mornings. We sit at the table and have toast and he explains it all. Over and over and over again. Me and him in another world. God, I should've said something.

MACMILLAN   He probably loved those moments as much
            as you did. Closeness. I remember when I
            was a tot my dad and I used to watch…

LORRAINE   But it's all tied in. The ray guns and force
            fields. That's straight from the story. I knew
            he believed it and I never said a word. And
            now Eliot's boosted the car and gone.

MACMILLAN   Mmm. And you've no idea why he hit the
            road? No? Probably just upset. Anything
            else? Anything that might help us cut to their
            destination?

*KEVIN enters carrying a tray of teas. He dishes them
out.*

LORRAINE   No. The Mother Ship swoops in from above,
            all lights and sound and whisks him away, but
            there's no set pick up point. His Skypod helps
            him track it you see, and when he does, they
            switch round.

MACMILLAN   Switch round?

LORRAINE   With the real Gerry. That's the story, the real
            Gerry was the boy who nearly drowned. The
            aliens took the real Gerry when he was in
            the coma and replaced him with the Gerry
            we have now, from the planet Nibiru. Alien
            Gerry. It's an exchange visit. That's why
            he's… Gerry says that's why he's different. In
            his mind he's not a kid with different abilities,
            because in his mind, he's not a kid at all. He's
            an alien here to study life as a young human.
            So when the Mother Ship comes, they switch
            round again. We get the…we get the real
            Gerry back.

KEVIN   What powers has he got?

LORRAINE   What are you still doing here?

47

KEVIN Not pressing assault charges and making tea.

LORRAINE sips her tea.

LORRAINE Aaaaaargh eeeew. God, what's in this?

KEVIN Oop. Sorry.

KEVIN switches her cup with MACMILLAN's. LORRAINE has dropped MACMILLAN's card from earlier. KEVIN picks it up.

What? It's sweeteners. Honestly it's sweeteners. Don't drink it then. Constable.

MACMILLAN Pardon?

KEVIN I said constable. Says on this card you're a double constable. Is that the truth and nothing but the truth?

MACMILLAN Yes.

KEVIN He admits it. Constable Constable's a constable. Thought as much.

MACMILLAN What are you…?

LORRAINE Ignore him Mac. Look, this is what I'm worried about: he thinks, because he's a Traveller (that's what the Aliens are called) that he's got powers. And if he's started acting them out he could get really hurt.

MACMILLAN What are the powers?

LORRAINE Well…

KEVIN Oh he gets an answer.

LORRAINE …he can walk on water, he can turn invisible, he can read minds, he can travel huge distances in a second, he can bamboozle people, I think he can fly, he can heal people, there's a stack of it. But the big one is that he's going to bring us all together and save the world.

MACMILLAN   Wow. This is…wow.

LORRAINE   I knew this would happen. I knew I should've said something, one of those mornings. It would've been natural for a real mother. But he was grown up when I met Jim and it was already part of him. And…and okay, I've struggled. I've never been at ease with it. With the way people looked at him. The pity in the street. But Gerry didn't see those looks, he didn't even sense them I don't think, because he had this story. He knew the truth. So he was bullet-proof. And who would take that away? Not me.

MACMILLAN   No. Not me.

KEVIN   I would've. I'd've told him straight. Listen you little hosepipe, you're talking crap. Apart from Michael Jackson, aliens don't exist. What?

LORRAINE   Kevin I want you to go.

KEVIN   Why?

LORRAINE   Because you're a little boy.

KEVIN   I'm not.

LORRAINE   You are. You're a little boy who lives a little boy's life. You have a little boy's job that you'll probably have for the rest of your days. And no matter what little boy nonsense you talk, or how sharp you assume you are, you're useless in any real situation and I don't think you'll ever make a man. And I can't cope with another little boy just now.

This hits KEVIN hard. He looks like a little boy right enough. He starts to go but MACMILLAN's radio barks into life.

MACMILLAN Go ahead.

Some racy staccato sounds that we can't make out.

We've got him.

He and LORRAINE bustle out in a gasp. After a moment of thinking time. KEVIN follows.

11

The Liberator stutters to a stop, the freshly bought L-Plates lost in the fumes. JUDY struggles with a map, ELIOT struggles with his temper. They are exactly in the middle of nowhere.

ELIOT Apparently L-plates only work if the person in the passenger seat knows what they're doing.

JUDY I know what I'm doing.

ELIOT Yeah but…

JUDY And don't start with your assumptions mate, I can drive, I just need hand controls.

ELIOT It's the map reading that's in question.

JUDY Did someone tell you that women like sarcastic little swines or is it something you're working on all by yourself?

ELIOT I… I… I…

JUDY Apology accepted. This is weird. We should be there. We did everything right. Look.

ELIOT   I've been up here a million times. None of this rings any bells. We need a Skypod.

JUDY   A what?

ELIOT   Oh it's from a game me and Gerry would play. Aliens. One of their powers is that they can shift the world around so no one can find them. The only way to get where you're going is to use a Skypod.

JUDY   And when did you play this game?

ELIOT   When we were little.

JUDY   But after iPods came out right?

ELIOT   Let me see that map. Those trees shouldn't be there.

JUDY   Have you got a girlfriend?

ELIOT   Eh?

JUDY   Have you got a girlfriend?

ELIOT   No.

JUDY   Have you ever had a girlfriend?

ELIOT   Yes.

JUDY   Who?

ELIOT   You wouldn't know them.

JUDY   How do you know?

ELIOT   You don't go to my school.

JUDY   What's her name?

ELIOT   I'm not telling you.

JUDY   It's because she's fictional isn't it?

ELIOT   No.

JUDY   She's one of those fictional people isn't she? A made up kind of gal. An invisible type. Have you ever kissed someone?

ELIOT   Shut up, look in case you haven't noticed…

JUDY   Somebody real I mean. With their full consent.

ELIOT   I'm not going to tell you anything about anything, I swear to God…

JUDY   Okay okay. Chill. I just wondered what it was like that's all. Research purposes. It looks good.

After a moment or two.

ELIOT   I think we're going to have to double-back to the main road and re-try.

JUDY   It's getting quite dark.

ELIOT   We'll go back a bit, find the road, fire over to the Christmas tree place, pick up Gerry and then…well I dunno…head back I suppose. We'll be long home by sundown.

JUDY   The sun's going down now is what I'm saying.

ELIOT   Well…just don't mention it.

JUDY   Don't mention it and therefore it won't happen. Excellent plan. Is that what you're doing with your exam results? Hoping that if you keep them in the envelope and don't look, then over time the grades will rise? Like bread in an oven?

ELIOT   I don't need to look. I know how I did. You talk a lot of crap know that. You think you're all smart and cool but really you're just a…

JUDY I know. I know what I really am.

Pause. ELIOT feels like a shit. Change of subject.

ELIOT Right. Well. We'd better get going. So…eh…
you going to write about this? Put me in one
of your stories?

JUDY No way.

ELIOT No way?

JUDY No way. I write fan fiction. Online. Stories
based on *Buffy* or *Charmed* or *Pirates of The
Caribbean.*

ELIOT What's the point in that?

JUDY What's the point of a car that turns into a
boat? Some things don't have points.

ELIOT So you just re-write the scripts?

JUDY No, I give them completely new stories. I
make them romantic. Every story I write
is a romance and usually builds to a very
tastefully done sex scene. They're very
popular on the internet.

ELIOT I'll bet they are.

JUDY It's not porn. It's romance. Boys have always
had a difficulty telling the difference between
the two so don't feel too bad.

ELIOT Here, grab the map. You're the navigator.

JUDY Then you have Gerry's painting. I can't hold
both.

ELIOT Hey there's words on this.

JUDY I told you that.

ELIOT Does that…that says…

JUDY Is it the name of the Christmas tree place?

ELIOT No. I don't know what it is. But it's weird.
This is the second time I've heard of it today.

JUDY What does it say? I couldn't make it out.

ELIOT It says… 'The House Of Light'.

12

KEVIN is fulfilling the birthright of his generation.

He's on TV.

And he's deliberately using his MAN-voice.

KEVIN Well Mandy, I think the term 'Extraterrestrial Superbeing ' is over-used, but yes, in this case, that's exactly what we're dealing with here. This boy is pretty trucking certain that he's a superpowered alien, and who are we to argue? He seems to be returning to his Mother Ship in a blaze of glory reminiscent of *Independence Day* or to a lesser extent, the bits at the beginning of *War Of The Worlds* before it gets rubbish. Hopefully though, it won't end with the worldwide slaughtering of innocents. Although obviously, it is still too early to say.

Yes, some people will presume that he's just labouring under massive delusions and should be provided with as much care as the law can muster, but that's what they said about Girls Aloud and look at them now.

Well I am simply a very, very close friend of the family, whose deepest wish is to see young Gerry returned to his loving stepmother's smooth, smooth arms and that is why I'm making this plea on bog standard regional television in the hope of national syndication. I think it's what any MAN would do in this situation. I should also say that I've set up a website dedicated to the hunt, www.findthislittlealien.com which has a link to my MySpace page as well as the already legendary YouTube posting of me in tears pleading for Gerry's life that is excellent. Heart-breaking of course, but excellent. Eighteen views already. Favourited once.

Oh right, yeah, as I was saying, I've come to a MAN's decision. And that is to make an appeal to any Sci-Fi fan, any UFO spotter, any alien hunter out there, to help us find Gerry and his wayward pals. Look at it this way; if he's not an alien, you'll be helping a very special kid find his way home. But if he *is* an alien, and all the reports of his powers are true, then you'll have a front row seat at the event of the century. Think on losers.

Thank you Mandy, and who knows, perhaps you and I shall be talking again when my court case against Mr Toadheath of Sundrenched Leisure and Care facilities comes up. Unless they make a suitable offer of course.

13

LORRAINE is stunned to stop, pinned to the spot: her name is heckled by reporters, her arm pulled. Bright camera lights are like planets, orbiting her. Without knowing it, she puts her hands across her belly, protecting her unborn child from the universe of THIS that swarms around her.

MACMILLAN, looking a lot more like a proper policeman now, steers the horde away, or steers LORRAINE away from the horde, anything to get a private word with her. They are at the entrance to Lonesome Pines farm, the Christmas tree place.

MACMILLAN   It's worse inside. We've just nicked a guy dressed as Gandalf climbing the fence packing a Stanley blade, and three Klingons who say if we don't let Gerry go there'll be repercussions.

LORRAINE   You've got Gerry? Where is he?

MACMILLAN   No that's the thing. He was gone before we turned up. But with all this, it was impossible to know the score. The crowds tailed the TV crews and they tailed us.

LORRAINE   I'm going to kill that Kevin. Kill him!

MACMILLAN   He probably just thought it was the right thing to do.

LORRAINE   I swear to God, if someone definitely knew the right thing to do now I'd kiss them very hard on the mouth. We should say *that* on TV. Or maybe not. Might put them off.

MACMILLAN   Yeah it's em…well it's all under control. We've got tracks from the van and there's some CCTV on the junction we're looking at. We'll have them very very soon. I'm…

eh…I'm on the case, as we say in the force. Definitely.

LORRAINE   So what are we still doing here then? Let's go!

MACMILLAN   We can't. Not yet. This could get out of control. Containment's the name of the game. There's a bit of an incident in there and if Gandalf and his hobbit posse get wind they'll freak. And Klingons are a warring people, so bloodshed's never far away when they're about.

LORRAINE   What is it?

MACMILLAN   It's just always been a part of their nature, they're a confrontational race. In fact their planet Kronos was at one time…

LORRAINE   Are you serious? Are you taking the piss? Because if you are I swear to God…

MACMILLAN   No! No I'm sorry. I wouldn't. I'm just a bit of a fan that's all. It all gets mixed up sometimes.

LORRAINE   So what's going on in there?

MACMILLAN   The media, if they so much as…

LORRAINE   Mac. Please.

MACMILLAN   There's a field of little pine trees. They sell them at Christmas time. As of yesterday, hunky-dory. But now…

LORRAINE   What?

MACMILLAN   See with hay or wheat, there's an explanation apparently, but trees; the guy reckons it would take three kids a week just to…

LORRAINE   Mac!

MACMILLAN   It's a crop circle. Well not a circle exactly.

LORRAINE Then what is it?

MACMILLAN It's more like a diagram. A pattern. Like an arrow, or a tower or…or…here look.

MACMILLAN struggles to explain, so he gets a stick and draws it on the ground beneath them. It is exactly like that thing in GERRY's painting. And he's right; it could be a tower; it could be an arrow; it could be a triangle. It could even be a Christmas tree. There are lines coming from the point at the top. Like a call of light.

14

There's no denying it now: it's dark.

ELIOT's freezing and searching at speed under the seats for something – anything!

JUDY takes turns looking from the map to ELIOT's bum which pokes up dumbly as he scrambles.

ELIOT Ah…ah…ah ha! AH HA!

JUDY What you got?

ELIOT It's a…oh. I thought it was a Lion Bar.

JUDY What is it?

ELIOT I don't know. Something…something soggy with lumps. Eew. I think it's bleeding.

JUDY Well you've achieved your goal. I'm no longer hungry.

ELIOT God it's cold. I'm so cold.

JUDY I think I've pinpointed the exact point on the map where we went wrong. Look. Here.

ELIOT That's where we started off.

JUDY   Yeah. We should never have started off. What we going to do?

ELIOT   Keep going, what else? I mean somewhere they'll be a sign or a farm or garage or something man. There has to be. Like, logic dictates.

JUDY   We haven't seen anything in hours. Where are we?

ELIOT   You'd think we'd be on the other side of England by now. This is impossible.

JUDY   Is there any chance we've been driving in circles?

ELIOT   You're the one with the map.

JUDY   Let me rephrase the question. Is there any chance you've been deliberately driving in circles?

ELIOT   Why would I do that?

JUDY   I don't know.

ELIOT   Well, no. There isn't. I haven't.

JUDY   No. Didn't think so.

ELIOT   He'll be home by now eh? Bound to be.

JUDY   No joy from the mobile?

ELIOT   Deader than whatever that is under my seat.

JUDY   I wonder what my mum and dad are thinking? Wonder if they've even noticed. Doubt they're on the hunt. Not like you. Don't worry, he'll be home by now. He's a sensible kid really. Underneath.

ELIOT   I dunno about that. It's 100 per cent gibber some nights.

JUDY   He's so funny man. The impressions.

ELIOT   Oh my God.

JUDY   It's a scream. Do you think he knows how
        bad they are?

ELIOT   Of course he does, that's the point. Daft idiot.
        Makes me giggle though.

JUDY   When he does his little…

ELIOT   Yeah. Idiot.

Thinking about GERRY they both laugh a little.

        He's good though. He's good.

JUDY   Do you think this is him just like, gasping for
        attention or something?

ELIOT   No. It's not. I think… I think… It's about
        getting back to what it was like before.

JUDY   Before what?

ELIOT   You know what happened.

JUDY   No. You don't ask. There's not always a story.
        Most times it's just like, the way it is. The way
        it's always been. Know what I mean.

ELIOT   It wasn't always this way. Not for him.
        Funny, he was doing an impression then
        too. Honestly. Guess who he was doing an
        impression of just before he went under?
        Guess.

JUDY   I don't…

ELIOT   Take a guess.

JUDY   I really d…

ELIOT   Jesus. He was doing an impersonation of
        Jesus. So funny, man. Lake District as always.

Coniston, as always. By that little island.
Bobbing on the water in this thing and we're
swimming and he's doing Jesus impressions.
We had the arm bands on, floating out and
out, and Dad was sitting here writing a letter
to Mum. She was dead in her grave by then,
but that's what he did when we went places.
So we swam out. Leaving all that stuff in here.
We both had a blue rope tied round our waist,
knotted to the door. So he could get to us.
Right here. See. Gerry's further than out than
me shouting

15

GERRY Eliot, I'm deeper than you. I'm always deeper
than you.

ELIOT No it's deeper back here.

GERRY Go under.

ELIOT I've done that hundreds of times man.

GERRY Go under then. Dive the deep dive.

ELIOT Shut up.

GERRY You're scared to go under.

ELIOT No I'm not I'm

*GERRY goes under. ELIOT gets to his brother's rope and
pulls it. Nothing. Getting worried. GERRY reappears
further away, laughing, harder to make out now.*

Come back Gerry, I'm telling Dad.

GERRY I'm still on the rope. You can always get
to me.

ELIOT Yeah but…

GERRY Don't be scared my son. I will heal you of your worries. I will miracle you all better with my powers. The power of the Lord will show you the way under water you scaredy big soft girly girl!

ELIOT (*Laughing.*) Shut up dickhead. I can go under any time I want.

GERRY Want to see an impression?

ELIOT Seen it. Father Archie. Very good. I'm going back. Too cold.

GERRY takes off his arm-bands.

Keep the arm-bands on man! Dad says you've to keep them on.

GERRY Duh! I can totally swim. Here, watch this. Who's this?

GERRY puts the arm-bands on his feet and tries to stand up in the water.

Check it, I'm walking on water! Eliot! I've put the arm bands on my feet look. I'm walking on water, honest. Check it out! I'm the big man. Jeezy Creezy! Amen! Amen! Halleluiah brother!

ELIOT's laughing like crazy.

I've got a joke right. What's the difference between Jesus and

GERRY flips over in the water, his feet always pulled to the surface by the arm-bands. Struggle and splash and foam and arm and gasp and no, under again.

ELIOT watches it. Knowing for certain now that time is drowning away and that this is wrong wrong wrong.

*Go under! Save him! Shout! Something. Now is the time
for something. No. He just watches until the water is
nearly still and the rope is yanked with the might and
the screams of a father.*

*As GERRY fades from sight. ELIOT is pulled back to the
Amphicar. Back to*

16

ELIOT   'Course the arm bands kept pushing him
upside down. Kept him under water.
And by the time dad pulled him back that
was it. Dad didn't pull me back at all.

A long, long silence. To change the subject…

JUDY   So. Are you looking forward to having a new
brother or sister?

ELIOT   What do you mean? It's not real. The old
Gerry's not coming back, you know that
don't you? He's the same Gerry! It was Gerry
then, it's Gerry now and it's Gerry for ever
and ever. He's gonna be like this till the very
end and he has to get that through his thick,
moonster skull. There's no magic switcherroo.
There's no Mother Ship swooping in to save
him! There's no nothing doing nothing. It's
just day after day after day of this. 'Cos see
all that stuff, it's ripping me up man. Every
word of it, ripping me up. It's just a story. It
always was. How was I to know he'd to cling
to it, like bloody blue rope? Why didn't it
just fade and go like everything else? Why is
it this that's left? This stupid, tiny story from
the top of my head. But oh no, everything
I do is cursed to stick, everything I do ends

in some…storm. Do nothing: storm. Do
something: storm. And after the storm,
everything's gone and I'm to blame. I was
trying to… I was *trying* to…but I couldn't. I
didn't. I just didn't.

*Another long silence. JUDY lets ELIOT pull it back.
Quietly, carefully…*

JUDY   I meant are you looking forward to the baby?

ELIOT   Oh. Oh right. I haven't really thought
about it.

JUDY   Is it a boy or a girl?

ELIOT   No one knows.

JUDY   What would you prefer?

ELIOT   I dunno. A girl maybe. A sister.

JUDY   My favourite name for a girl is Bo.

ELIOT   Bo. Bo? How do you spell that?

JUDY   B O.

ELIOT   You want to call a kid B O?

JUDY   You're going to say it stinks right?

ELIOT   *I* won't say it. The kids beating her up in
the playground every single day'll say it,
absolutely, but me? Never.

*JUDY laughs a bit. ELIOT smiles despite himself. Wipes
his eyes.*

I made up a story about Gerry and he…

JUDY   The Travellers. The aliens that took the old
Gerry and replaced him. I know. He told me.
I know about the Mother Ship too. And his
powers.

ELIOT Then why have you…?

JUDY I don't know. At the start I wanted to see how you'd react and by then it was too late. I'm a bit of a liar. I lie a lot actually.

ELIOT Yeah. Me too.

JUDY Hey you want to know something cool?

ELIOT What?

JUDY It's not your fault. Anything. Everything. It's not your fault.

Pause.

ELIOT Say it again.

JUDY It's not your fault.

In this pause they both realise that they quite like it here.

ELIOT It's so cold man. Can't feel my legs.

JUDY Snap.

ELIOT What, at all?

JUDY Some. Not much.

ELIOT What can you feel?

JUDY I couldn't feel this.

She pinches ELIOT on the leg.

ELIOT Ah! Can you feel this?

He pinches her calf.

JUDY No. Although I might feel this.

Punches his thigh, hard.

ELIOT Ah!

JUDY   But of course I couldn't be sure.

ELIOT   What about this. (*Nips her thigh.*) Feel that?

JUDY   See, you've not thought this through.

The laughing is gentle. ELIOT dives the deep dive.

ELIOT   Can you feel this?

Touches her arm.

JUDY   Yeah.

Pause.

ELIOT   Can you feel this?

Touches her face.

JUDY   Yes.

ELIOT   Can you feel…?

JUDY   Oh for God's sake.

They kiss. And so on.

17

The Homelight sweeps the world in a huge aching curve.

It sees everything this night has to offer as it goes on its powerful orbit, readying the landing spot for the Mother Ship.

It sees MACMILLAN, pouring over the videos, notes and maps. It doesn't make sense. There's nothing out there. The only place they could be heading is…no wait a minute he did read something about that place. Maybe…

It sees LORRAINE sitting on the edge of her bed, coat still on, lights still off. The tears on her cheeks are effortless, and she nearly doesn't notice the pain beginning. Her phone shoots light from her hand like a ray gun.

It sees KEVIN, alone in his room, lit by the TV news as it shows footage of LORRAINE at the Christmas tree field. Then there are people in costumes raving, roaming and hunting in huge numbers. Followers now, calmly flowing over the hills like fans at the end of a festival. There are claims of conversions and healings. Crutches are thrown to the ground and fingers point to the sky as they testify, dreamily.

The banner on the screen reads 'Reports of Alien Miracles'. One convert grabs the camera and is madly drawing a shape on paper for the reporter. The pattern reminds KEVIN of something. He pulls a ripped poster from his pocket.

The Homelight sees the Travellers. Loads of them, huddled round fires, listening to their leader as he preaches their history, detail by detail. He sweeps his arm and the stars explode in patterns and pictures. The night is his blackboard. Their eyes glow as he tells of his upcoming switch-round.

Space Mosquitoes arrive one by one, lighting the way for the massive Mother Ship, pulling itself closer and closer. It's far away now but it's coming.

We can feel its brilliant light, warm on our face, we can feel its distant roar, gentle on our skin.

Closer, closer, closer.

Now long now.

And finally the light covers The Liberator in sweeping beats.

It can't see JUDY and ELIOT though. Nobody can. The roof has been put up. Inside they are shivering and delighted in each other's arms, waiting behind misted windows, for the new morning.

18

The morning, when it comes, is cold and wild. When KEVIN's cab draws away he pulls his sweatshirt hood up over his head and studies the poster again. This can't be it can it?

When he sees the Amphicar parked outside, like it's been there all night, his mouth falls open.

He circles it. No doubt. This is ELIOT's car! What the hell's it doing here?

He peers in through the clouded windows.

It takes a scream from inside to bounce him back. The door flies open and ELIOT flies out, flies open.

ELIOT What the hell you doing man?

KEVIN What the hell am *I* doing, what the hell are *you* doing?

ELIOT What do you think I'm doing?

KEVIN I don't know. I couldn't see. Who's in there? Gerry?

ELIOT (*Blocking his view into the Amphicar.*) What are you doing here?

KEVIN Same as you.

ELIOT I doubt it mate. Listen…em…eh…look man…I…eh…

JUDY pokes her head up and locks eyes with KEV.
They both gasp. She ducks down and scrambles into
clothes & persona.

KEVIN   Is that…is that…no way man. Totally, totally
no way man. Dude!

ELIOT   Eh…em…right…okay…you know…shut
up. Believe it or not, I'm not looking for the
moral approval of a motherfunster.

KEVIN   You're calling me a motherfunster?

ELIOT   You *are* a motherfunster. Literally.

KEVIN   No way. She's not your mum and it was never
fun. Not even close.

ELIOT   Just get lost Kevin, me and you are over.

KEVIN   Hey guess what, that's what she said. Honest
man. There's nothing going on. There was
never anything going on. So you can chill.
She hates me. And I'm sorry. I am. I really
am. Look I know I've been a Phantom
Menace about this. A total butter merchant.
I've been an apple picker I know it, but…

ELIOT   Stop talking like that. Doing my head in. Just
walk away Kev. Walk away and keep walking.

KEVIN turns to go. He doubles back.

KEVIN   See it's alright for you, you know. You've
got Lorraine and Gerry and the new baby
and…and…a car that turns into a boat; and
soon you'll be away at university and have
an amazing, exciting life somewhere else, but
I won't. I've not got what you've got. This is
me for keeps man. I know it is. So she was
like…she was… I love her. And I can't help
it. And if that makes me a dick then I'm a
dick. But if *you* think I'm a dick…then that's it

for me. I've got nothing left. That's me done.
So.

He starts to walk away forlornly.

ELIOT Wait. Wait. (*With difficulty.*) I don't really think
you're a dick. No one does.

*The roof of the Amphicar comes down. JUDY seems much
more like her old self since we glimpsed her last.*

JUDY Hey look, it's that dick from the swimming
pool. Alright Dick?

ELIOT Ignore her she's a…

KEVIN She's a…

ELIOT Honest to God Kevin.

KEVIN No, I was going to say…em… all those
'dicks' don't count. Right? I didn't want to
antagonise the situation further with my new
vocab. I'm all about the smooth over. You've
taught her to speak good by the way. And hey
is it definitely legal for you to…?

ELIOT Kev, the ice couldn't be thinner mate. And
I really do owe you a massive slap from
yesterday, so keep going, please.

KEVIN No, no. Pals right? Right Eliot?

ELIOT Right. Just…you know…don't.

KEVIN I won't.

ELIOT Good. My God. You love Lorraine. Eeeew.

JUDY Who's Lorraine?

KEVIN His mum.

ELIOT Stepmum.

KEVIN   And don't slag her off. She's worried sick about this. She totally loves you. You're jammy to have that.

ELIOT   How did you get all the way out here?

JUDY   *Why* did you get all the way out here?

KEVIN   Toad's got a taxi account. Be a shame to waste it. And I told you, this is where Gerry is heading. Has to be, right? The House of Light. He's tagging the logo all over the shop. Remember the poster? See.

ELIOT and JUDY share a look. It's exactly like his painting.

'Virginity Now. A conference for all school leavers heading off to university to discuss the Christian ideal of abstinence.' The House of Light. It's a Christian retreat or something. Ironic eh?

ELIOT   How's it ironic?

KEVIN   Well. You two. Here.

JUDY   What's ironic about that? What on earth could be ironic about that Eliot? Have you been spreading the gospel?

ELIOT   I haven't said a word, he's... I don't know what he's on about. What you on about?

KEVIN   Nothing. Just. You know. You're right outside.

ELIOT   Outside what?

KEVIN   The House of Light! Check it.

They do. Maybe mist clears, or maybe they just never thought to look up, but KEVIN's right. They're right outside –

JUDY   A lighthouse.

This is what GERRY had been trying to draw.

ELIOT This looks kind of, familiar.

KEVIN I know. From Gerry's clues. It's not a lighthouse anymore though. Now it's where virgins go.

JUDY For what?

KEVIN Conferences, and then, I presume, sex.

ELIOT Wait a minute. We're at the coast?

JUDY How did we…?

ELIOT We couldn't've! We were a hundred miles away. At least! Not unless…

KEVIN You're right on the beach man, look. Sweet parking.

JUDY I need to get out. This is too weird.

ELIOT Give us a minute eh?

KEVIN No worries. Fire in.

ELIOT Alone.

KEVIN Oh. Okay. Cool. I'll em… I'll case the joint.

KEVIN reluctantly leaves them behind as he scopes out the lighthouse, occasionally glancing over his shoulder as he disappears from view.

During the following JUDY pulls out her chair from the back of the Amphicar, sets it up and lifts herself into it.

JUDY So.

ELIOT So.

JUDY An official good morning to you.

ELIOT Morning.

JUDY   Horrible isn't it?

ELIOT   Horr…? Well. Y…

JUDY   The weather.

ELIOT   Oh. Right. Absolutely. Storm's a-coming.
Look I never said anything to Kevin. I
wouldn't.

JUDY   Are you ashamed?

ELIOT   No.

JUDY   Cold light of day. Wondering what people
will think? It's only natural.

ELIOT   No.

JUDY   It's okay. Honestly. Well…was it really ironic?
You know. Being right outside. For you?

ELIOT   You mean was it my…?

JUDY   Because it was ironic for me. You probably
guessed.

ELIOT   No. I didn't. You were…know what I mean. It
didn't seem ironic. But…it was. For me. Too.
It was.

JUDY   Was it?

ELIOT   Totally.

JUDY   What about the euphemism you had in your
wallet?

ELIOT   The what? Oh the euphemism. No, Kev gave
it to me for a Christmas present. I think it was
a joke.

JUDY   A practical joke, as it turns out.

ELIOT   Yeah. Look I'm sorry.

JUDY What for?

ELIOT I don't know. This just feels like one of those times when apologies are due. I don't mean… I didn't mean…oh I'd better shut my face before I do some real damage. Look maybe when we get Gerry back and it all goes normal again we can, you know, go to the cinema or go ice skating or…

JUDY is in the chair now and ELIOT's face falls. She catches his expression and her heart cracks just a little bit.

JUDY Yeah. Maybe.

KEVIN comes running back on.

KEVIN Something's going down. ET's in the building and he's mob-handed! Aliens v God. There can be only one victor! Let's get ready to rumble!

19

In a police car nee-nawing at speed round coastal roads in the rain. LORRAINE clings to her seat and MACMILLAN's translating the coded barks coming from the radio.

MACMILLAN No one can tell if the Aliens have the Christians trapped or if it's the Christians that have got the Aliens trapped, but the doors are locked from the inside and we've had reports of laser fire *and* piercing beams of heavenly light, so it's all kicking off one way or another.

LORRAINE What about Gerry?

MACMILLAN He's got to be there hasn't he, he's the leader.

LORRAINE   He's just a little boy.

MACMILLAN   The TV swines are present and correct, as
are about 300 morons with placards. What
amazes me is how they got there before us,
it's in the middle of nowhere. It's like they
just stepped out of the storm. Either that or…
No. I tell you, if this thing does turn up we're
going to have pandemonium on our hands.

LORRAINE   What thing? The Mother Ship! You're
seriously thinking that… Mac it's not real.
Aliens aren't real. It's crazy.

MACMILLAN   How do you know? No, really? 'Cos if you
ask me, it's more likely that aliens exist than
some big beardy God sitting on a cloud
judging us and sending us all to hell for being
different, but nobody says believing in God is
crazy. Everyone's got to believe in something.
Something that makes all the rubbish
worthwhile. And I want this to be true. I
really do. I feel it's true. In my chest. I've felt
it there since I was a kid.

LORRAINE   Mac…

MACMILLAN   I know what you're going to say but witnesses
swear they saw lights swirling around the
Travellers, and I've spoken to three people
who have actually been cured.

LORRAINE   Mac…

MACMILLAN   And okay two of those had matching head
wounds but one woman swears she had crabs
yesterday and now they're gone and ask
yourself, why would she lie? This might be it.
This might be the day the stories come true.

LORRAINE   Mac I'm having the baby.

MACMILLAN What?

LORRAINE Don't stop. Get to Gerry.

MACMILLAN Are you sure? It's coming now?

LORRAINE Now. Right, right, right now. Keep driving.

MACMILLAN We've got to go back to town.

LORRAINE No! It's too far. My children are at the end of this road. Please. Don't turn back.

The car skids to a stop. After a moment.

MACMILLAN No. Look I'm sorry Lorraine but it's an about-turn. I can radio for an ambulance to meet us but we're miles out. Even if I set the sirens loud and blast off, it's going to take an hour tops, so we have to get a move on. Or…

LORRAINE Please God don't be adding 'ors' at this late stage in the game.

MACMILLAN Or…*or*…there's a tiny medical room about a mile from here. It's in the building where I do my lessons. (*A horrified look from LORRAINE.*) Yes! They've got a nurse and a cabinet full of stuff.

LORRAINE A cabinet full of …

MACMILLAN Listen! This is the right thing to do. Definitely. Trust me. I'll still get your boys back don't worry. But until then, just buckle up and breathe.

LORRAINE You'll miss the Mother Ship.

MACMILLAN I'd rather see the baby land safe and sound.

LORRAINE Really?

MACMILLAN Yeah. Plus I'm taping the news, just in case.

LORRAINE You're…weird.

MACMILLAN Maybe. But I'm a wicked driver. Hold on tight. Houston we have lift off!

The car screeches off in a U-turn of smoke and siren.

20

No matter what they think outside

Inside the Homelight

Everything's fine.

The Travellers are excited and safe,

And the others want to help, not hurt.

One tribe, not two.

Hands are held.

Eyes glow.

And there's music, building from down low

Drowning out the storm whirling

Round and round and rising.

One last job to do.

A hero in the middle, smiling and strong.

Patted and hugged, remembered for this, no matter what comes next.

But it's time now.

Check the Skypod and activate the lightcast.

A zap of energy to the bulb of the Homelight.

Yaaaaaaaays as the big beam is shone, huge and strong

Out and onto the cold grey sea.

They think they're at the end of their journey.

All of them. Travellers and Pray-ers

They think that now the locks can unlock, and the game can be dropped. Safe and sound. No harm done. This is further than they ever thought they'd come.

But they're wrong. It's not finished yet. Not for everyone.

As the crowd celebrates the end of whatever it was for them

Two eyes close.

Turn invisible.

Disappear and glide out.

The Homelight points the way

Of course it does

To the pick-up point

And the Mother Ship.

21

Battling through the crowds of cops and gawkers but getting nowhere, ELIOT, JUDY and KEVIN re-group outside the lighthouse, the sea wind blasting them back, forcing them to shout and sway in the storm.

ELIOT We've got to get in there!

KEVIN Guy says they've got it locked from the inside. The Christians were worried some of these mad banjos were going to hurt Gerry and his pals.

JUDY   Who *are* these people?

KEVIN   Alien hunters, sci-fi divots, duckwits that think the end of the world is nigh.

ELIOT   What are they all doing here? How did they hear about this?

KEVIN   Em…probably the internet? You know what it's like. It's a loser zoo at the best of times. This is out of order though eh? Someone should do something.

JUDY   Tell them that he's your brother, they might let you…

The high beam from the lighthouse flips on with a CHUNG. They shield their eyes. ELIOT remembers…

ELIOT   This is it.

JUDY   What?

ELIOT   This is the end. This is what's supposed to happen.

JUDY   Wait a minute. Don't tell me you're starting to believe all this are you?

ELIOT   Well how else did we get here? How did Gerry get here? All these people. This is happening. I don't understand it, but it is.

JUDY   It's not though.

ELIOT   How can you say that? How can you honestly say, for absolute certain, that this has nothing to do with the Mother Ship. Are you that… arrogant?

JUDY   Are you? You can't just dodge reality by losing yourself in stories. It's not real.

ELIOT   You can talk. That's what you do. Fan fiction! You spend your nights making Harry and

Hermione get off with each other. For what? It's make-believe and you know it. You're hiding from the real world like everyone else. You're worse than me.

JUDY What's that under your shirt Eliot? That envelope. Looks like exam results. So don't start. You don't even have the guts to see how badly you've done. You can't face what comes next so you just ignore it. Now that's what I call hiding from the real world.

ELIOT takes out the envelope and rips it open. Without looking he hands it to JUDY.

ELIOT Three As. Right?

JUDY Three As.

KEVIN Three As!

JUDY Why would you…?

ELIOT Because I don't want to go! No one's ever asked me what *I* want to do. I don't want to move away and meet new people and do all that stuff everyone says will change my life. I don't want my life to change anymore. Why don't they get that? I don't want to leave home. The only people I've got left are there. Everyone else is lost. So you're right, I can't face what comes next. Unless what comes next is the Mother Ship. Because then all bets are off. And maybe then all those lost people will…maybe they'll…

JUDY Eliot. Listen. Listen. I'm sorry but the Mother Ship isn't bringing anyone back. Because it is not real. But this other stuff, all this scary stuff, it is. And in the end you'll have to look it in the eye and move on. That's what life is. And before you say it, of course I know the fan fiction is just make-believe, but I thought 'make-believe' was the best I could get. Real romance is for famous faces right? Not for me. Then it was last night. And I thought again. But now it's daylight and hey, I've looked the truth in the face and I'm dealing with it. Like I have to do every single day. And I know I'll probably never see you again after this. But last night it was real. It was proof. Like that impossible picture of your mum and dad in the Amphicar you told me about. Proof.

ELIOT is caught between tenderness and argument and is about to launch into one or the other when it hits him…

ELIOT The picture. That picture. That's it! The picture! The picture of mum and dad in the Amphicar on their first date. They were out on the sea and there's a pier in the background and…and a spotlight…coming from a lighthouse. This lighthouse! This is it! This is where the picture was taken!

KEVIN Eliot.

ELIOT How did he know where to find it?

KEVIN Eliot.

ELIOT Dad must've told him.

KEVIN Eliot.

ELIOT No. (*Smiling.*) It was Lorraine. Lorraine told him. Of course she did. I need to talk to Gerry.

KEVIN Well you might need to speak up. Look. There. Out at sea. Check it! That's him innit. He's heading for the light.

ELIOT Jesus Christ. Gerry! Jesus Christ.

JUDY Get the cops! Get the coastguard! 999.

ELIOT No. I can reach him. This time. I can save him this time.

KEVIN To the Carboat! Let's trucking rock and roll!

ELIOT Not you.

KEVIN Eh?

ELIOT I'm sorry man.

KEVIN Oh come on man let me go.

ELIOT This is a real situation Kev. We've not got time for any of your…sorry mate. Just us.

And they go.

KEVIN But… I'm a lifeguard.

KEVIN is left behind, sea-swept and stuck. This is the type of thing LORRAINE was on about wasn't it? A man would know what to do.

Then he remembers. Scrambling in his pocket – does he still have it? Yeah. MACMILLAN's card. He gets out his phone and dials.

22

The charging waves look like they've got the better of The Liberator, heaving it up and nearly over, sending sparks of spray into the sky and onto the faces of ELIOT and JUDY.

But no, down it goes, strongly fighting back against the squall.

It doesn't take them long to get close to GERRY.

He's in a small rowing boat losing his own battle with the storm. Both boats are heading for the fixed beam of the lighthouse: a bright white circle on the sea between them.

When The Liberator comes close enough it's clear to see that GERRY's lost control. As the sea takes over the decision-making, the determination that's brought him this far falls away and he screams. The oars slip from his hands and he's thrown off balance.

ELIOT is shouting and waving, trying to get his attention but it's no good.

The Liberator steers like a light log and seems to veer away when it should be closing the gap.

ELIOT Gerry! Gerry!

Finally GERRY hears and reacts; a small, unsurprised wave.

GERRY I'm scared Eliot.

ELIOT Gerry stay there. Hold on I'm coming.
Goddamn this thing I can't get close enough.

JUDY Give me the wheel.

ELIOT What?

JUDY Give me the wheel. I can do it. You reach for him.

They switch seats. ELIOT stands up in the Amphicar reaching for GERRY's hand.

Both boats are swirling around the bright centre of light.

ELIOT Gerry listen to me, you have to reach. You have to reach out!

GERRY I'm scared.

ELIOT Nothing's going to happen to you, I promise, just reach!

GERRY Where is it?

ELIOT What?

GERRY Where is it? Where is it?

ELIOT Gerry listen to me, you have to…

GERRY Yeah. I have to…maybe I have to…

GERRY stands up in his boat.

ELIOT Yeah that's it. Reach for me. Do it.

GERRY Do it?

ELIOT Do it!

Once last glance at his brother, a smile, and GERRY jumps from the boat into the sea, disappearing from sight under the waves.

No! Gerry!

JUDY Can you see him? Is he there? Can you see him? Eliot? Where is he?

ELIOT He's gone under. He gone…he's…

There's a beat before JUDY realises that ELIOT's frozen again. He's back at GERRY's accident. Same position, same terror, same thing. She knows that now is the time for…something.

JUDY Eliot. You know what to do. You do. You have to dive the deep dive. Dive the deep dive.

Without looking at her, without anything, he stands straight, and leaps from the Amphicar.

He goes under.

23

And under

And under

And under

Down here the world is black.

The struggling beams from the lighthouse weakly split the dark like arrows into smoke.

ELIOT swims down with all his might, away from the light, deeper towards GERRY.

GERRY is panicking, sinking and tumbling. His eyes are wide and white, his body desperate to give up the fight.

Until

The brothers see each other.

A burst of hope and effort.

They push towards each other with every scratch of life in their skin.

No. The drift sweeps them apart…it can't happen.

Get ready to say goodb…NO.

DIVE THE DEEP DIVE

One last surge of strength. One last launch.

And they will come together.

Yes! They do.

Grab each other. Hold.

Now it's all ELIOT: kicking, fighting, pushing, pushing,

to light, to air, to anything.

But GERRY holds him down. Fighting to stay under.

Eye to eye but never understanding. Why's he doing this?

And then, in a shoal of air bubbles, in a flash of panic, with a fast, sad, fading grip... .

GERRY drowns.

ELIOT doesn't open his mouth to scream.

Doesn't close his eyes.

Doesn't even look away.

Because now he gets it.

Yes. This is supposed to happen. This is how it ends.

So he gives up too.

Holding his brother, together they sink. Waiting.

Waiting.

Waiting.

Wait...

The sea shakes. The world shifts.

Now the universe is nothing except a monumental crescendo: a cacophony.

Now the galaxy is made entirely of light.

Because now...

It's here.

The Mother Ship.

A boom born on another planet banishes the entire ocean from them.

Vast pillars of colour bind them together.

ELIOT reaches out to the light, to the ray that will save them.

And when contact is made

The Mother Ship, filling the sky with swirling, whizzing, blasts of sound, lifts the brothers from the darkness

Up

Up

And away.

24

Up in the helicopter all hell is breaking loose.

It's hard to tell who's freaking out the most, KEVIN or MACMILLAN. KEVIN works the spotlight and the winch on instinct alone, while MACMILLAN flies the thing with the composure of a learner driver on the Champs Elysées.

They shout over the roar and the wind and the headphones.

KEVIN   Down, down down. There! Hold it. Hold it!

MACMILLAN   I can't do it if you shout! Speak calmly!

KEVIN   Hold it! Hold it right there!

MACMILLAN   Hurry up, I'm losing my shit here. I'm one wobble away from a puke.

KEVIN   Watch your language.

MACMILLAN   I'm going to be sick.

KEVIN   I can see them! Yes! They're there.

MACMILLAN   What do I do, what do I do?

KEVIN   Settle your stomach and hold it steady ya Constable…just… Hold! That's it. Right!

They're hooked on. Hold. They're on. Lift
off! Lift off! Lift off! Go go go!

*And with every fibre of strength and concentration,
MACMILLAN pulls the chopper up, up and away.*

*And exploding from the sea, the brothers are rocketed
into the sky. Clipped to the ladder, ELIOT holds GERRY
tight*

As they vanish into the stars.

25

In a corridor outside the medical room of the airstrip.

Shoulder to shoulder. Stunned and silent

Sit ELIOT and GERRY.

*Wrapped in towels and other people's clothes, it would
be hard to say for certain which one of them was dead
an hour ago.*

After ages…

ELIOT Kevin gave you mouth to mouth. Lip to lip.
What do you think of that? In some countries
that would mean you and him were married.
Eh? I couldn't believe it. I mean, I know he's
a lifeguard but I never really thought he'd
actually be able to, you know, do lifeguard
stuff. Just shows you.

A big silence with nothing in it.

I thought that was you, man. I thought you
were dead. Again.

GERRY You got me.

ELIOT Yeah.

GERRY I'm in trouble.

ELIOT Phhhft! Trouble? Too right. Jesus, you can say
that again. You were on the news man. Mind
you, you never know, you're famous now,
after it's all died down you might get rich.

GERRY That would be good.

ELIOT Be alright wouldn't it? (*Pause.*) How did you
get all those people following you? That's
the thing I don't understand. And they swear
blind they saw lights and lasers and that they
travelled through 'folds in time'. Some of
these guys are serious cases Gerry, you can't
just go about making them believe in stuff.
Their parents are raging.

GERRY You choose to believe. We all do that. Some
more than others.

ELIOT And what about the trees and the bus and all
the…

GERRY You know how it was done.

ELIOT The Mother Ship.

GERRY You know all about it.

ELIOT And you're going to sit there, recently dead,
telling me that you still believe in all that
crap?

GERRY I'm not dead anymore.

ELIOT So that makes it real?

GERRY What do you think?

ELIOT I think I made it up. All that moonster stuff. I
think you know that.

GERRY It worked.

ELIOT Look. I'm going to ask you something right? A favour. Just don't talk about it anymore. Face up to real life. Look it in the eye and move on. Okay? Because I'm going to be away after summer and I can't be stressing about you doing a bunk 'cos of some daft…

GERRY Okay.

ELIOT Okay?

GERRY Okay.

ELIOT You're not going to talk about it? The Travellers, the powers, the Mother Ship, this whole disaster?

GERRY No. It's over.

ELIOT The whole thing? Just like that.

GERRY It's done. Everything that was going to happen has happened. You can go now Eliot.

ELIOT What about…what about the switch round?

GERRY You can go. It all happened. But in a different way. A new way. It wasn't like we thought.

ELIOT Wasn't it?

GERRY It was better. Wait and see. Hey, I wonder if I'll get my own TV programme?

ELIOT I wonder.

GERRY I want one.

ELIOT Well you'll probably get one then, I think that's how it works. Gerry? Tell me. Honestly…was it real?

They look each other in the eye.

In come KEVIN and JUDY. KEVIN pushes JUDY's chair like an old pal. GERRY lights up when he sees her. Leaping to smother her in a cuddle.

GERRY Judy! Judy! Judy is my girlfriend.

JUDY Not really.

GERRY Me and Judy are getting married aren't we?

ELIOT Are you?

JUDY No.

GERRY Yes.

ELIOT Looks like I'm going to end up on Jeremy Kyle after all.

GERRY Did you see me in the sky?

JUDY I was a bit preoccupied.

ELIOT How's The Liberator?

JUDY Crashed.

ELIOT Cra...!

JUDY I'm fine until pedals are involved. Then I need hand controls and prevailing winds. In my defence, you were aware of that when you passed over command.

ELIOT So where is it?

JUDY Well it's not sunk. That's a fact. It is not sunk. Anymore. The police have got it. It'll be fine. Needs a bit of work. On the upside, a lot of people wanted to buy it. If you were selling that is.

ELIOT Well... You'll have to ask Gerry. It's his inheritance we've wrecked. What do you think mate? Should we say *bon voyage* to the Amphicar?

GERRY (*Thinking for a moment.*) No. I think we should keep it. It's ours now.

ELIOT Yeah, keep it. Hey maybe we could work on it? Make it new again. 'Cos it needs to be sooked-up and ship-shape for what I've got in mind.

JUDY Dare I ask…?

ELIOT Moonlit dates.

JUDY Eeew. Is that you being seductive?

ELIOT Maybe.

JUDY That needs work too. You're going to be busy.

GERRY What you two on about?

ELIOT Eh…

KEVIN Hey Gerry. I saved your life man. Mouth to mouth. In some countries…

ELIOT I've done that.

KEVIN Fair enough. I was on TV. I wonder if I'll get my own show. God I want one. Toad saw me. Says I'm promoted. I'm the new face of Sundrenched Leisure and Care Facilities marketing department. He's exploiting my new-found fame for his own financial gain and I don't care. I'm the new Hasselhoff.

JUDY That explains a lot.

KEVIN I'll be handing out leaflets probably, but hey, it's not forever.

GERRY Thank you Kevin.

ELIOT Yeah thanks Kev. Honestly. You're the man.

MACMILLAN comes out of the medical room.

MACMILLAN Okay boys she's ready to see you.

ELIOT, GERRY and KEVIN make for the door.

(*To KEVIN.*) Not you.

GERRY and ELIOT go through.

JUDY How is she constable?

MACMILLAN Oh she's wonderful. Wonderful. And eh… hate to be premature but…eh…speaking to the Guv there, I think I'm moving up. I don't think I'll be a constable for too much longer.

KEVIN Well I can honestly say, that to me, you'll always be a total and utter constable.

MACMILLAN Thank you Kevin. That's very nice of you. Here, what would you say if I was to suggest that you'd make a very fine policeman.

KEVIN Me?

MACMILLAN Yeah.

KEVIN I would say fuck right off. No!!

KEVIN slaps his hand across his mouth and falls to the ground in anguish. He'd come so far…

26

LORRAINE sits up in the hospital bed, cradling her new baby.

ELIOT and GERRY come in sheepishly.

LORRAINE My boys.

They sit on the bed. ELIOT carefully puts his arm around her. It's a while before anyone speaks.

ELIOT I'm sorry.

LORRAINE How did you get on? Three As right? Knew it. I'm so proud of you. Both. (*To GERRY.*) And you. Spaceboy. Anything to say to the new guy before we talk about this?

She hands him the baby. It takes GERRY a few moments to know how to phrase what he wants to say. But he gets there in the end.

GERRY Welcome home.

27

Miles above the world

Where the bright blue burns to black

And the stars are vast and wild

A space mosquito turns away

And sets a course for home.

And with a whirl and a flash

It's gone.

Lost to us in the glare of the sun

Racing from sight

Faster than light.

Faster than love.

THE END